WALK
LAKE I

Twenty-five
the Lak... District

WALKS IN THE LAKE DISTRICT

Twenty-five walks around the Lake District

Elizabeth Cull

———

COUNTRYSIDE BOOKS
NEWBURY, BERKSHIRE

First published by
Spurbooks 1979
© Elizabeth Cull 1979

This revised and updated Edition
Published 1990
© Elizabeth Cull 1990

COUNTRYSIDE BOOKS
3 Catherine Road
Newbury, Berkshire

ISBN 1 85306 107 7

Cover Photograph of Grasmere by Andy Williams

Publishers' Note
At the time of publication all footpaths used in these walks were designated as official footpaths or rights of way, but it should be borne in mind that diversion orders may be made from time to time.
Although every care has been taken in the preparation of this Guide, neither the Author nor the Publisher can accept responsibility for those who stray from the Rights of Way.

Produced through MRM Associates Ltd., Reading
Typeset by Acorn Bookwork, Salisbury,
Printed in England by J. W. Arrowsmith Ltd., Bristol

Contents

Introduction

The English Lake District is much smaller in area than you might imagine, being only thirty miles from West to East and twenty from South to North: a good walker might leave London by train early on a summer day, arrive in Windermere soon after noon and walk the length of High Street to be beyond Ullswater before nightfall, having traversed almost the whole of it. Far to the left along the way the Scafell range will have been in view, and far to the right the Pennines. With luck there will have been deer to see in Martindale and with extreme luck an eagle overhead above Riggindale crags. Rain or shine it will all have been memorable, and a magnificent start to a walking holiday.

But that is for experienced walkers, familiar with map and compass and with Cumbria and its ways. This book of Walks is meant for those who see these old hills for the first time and long to set foot on them, without quite knowing how or where to start. Here are safe routes to the heart of the high fells through which, in time, the whole district may be discovered.

On the fells distance takes second place to degree of difficulty. A mile of steep, craggy terrain can take three or four times longer than a mile tramped over level ground, so for some of the walks a time is given in place of a distance. Even times, though, must be approximate; some walkers will manage in less than the times given while others may take longer. You will quite soon discover which of these you are, and can judge your walking times accordingly.

Boots and clothing are important. Hardly any of these walks should be attempted without proper walking boots, or if that is not practicable then at least something with a good non-slip sole and high enough to support the ankle. Buy from a good Outdoor Shop, and if you cannot find anything locally to suit your pocket try writing to a mail order equipment shop. Remember when buying that you will be wearing a second pair of thick woollen socks on top of your usual walking socks to cushion the feet and prevent blisters, so buy boots at least one size larger than normal. Make sure they are really comfortable, not too heavy, and have a good, soft cuff around the ankle.

As with boots, so with clothing; the old padded anorak and jeans simply will not do for the Lake District. Jeans in particular should be avoided, as they cling to the legs when wet and do not dry readily in the wind. Wool of some sort is preferable, or cotton moleskin, or even ribbed nylon which remains warm when wet and quickly dries off when the rain stops. Until you experience it, you can have no conception of what rain can be like in Cumbria, so be prepared with lightweight over-trousers and a cagoule large enough to go over an anorak or over several layers of pullover, and long enough to sit on. I have tried various garments over the years advertised to keep the rain out, but haven't yet found anything to beat proofed nylon. It is cheap, easy to pack and carry, keeps the wind out and takes up minimal space in the rucksack, and you can re-proof it when necessary for less than the cost of a good pair of socks. After rain, the next great dampener is condensation inside the waterproofs. The best remedy for this, and for perspiration generally, is to wear natural fibre.

Apart from waterproofs, your kit should consist of a wool, cotton or brushed cotton shirt, two thin woollen pullovers sized for wearing in layers, and either a heavy pullover or a shower-proof anorak to wear on top. Gloves and a hat should always be carried, a piece of old, soft towelling to go around the neck in heavy rain is a good idea, as is a plastic bag inside the rucksack to keep reserve clothing dry. Never go out, even in summer, without this minimum kit; rain and cloud at 2,000 ft is COLD, and weather on the fells ever uncertain. A simple day sack is sufficient to carry these items, take advice from your supplier and choose one of good, waterproof quality, then try it on in the shop to be sure it is comfortable for you. It should be large enough to carry spare clothing and waterproofs, a packed lunch, thermos flask, glucose tablets, apples and oranges for thirst, and concentrated energy foods such as nuts, dried fruit or chocolate; dressings for blisters, spare bootlaces, tissues, a whistle for emergencies, and, absolute necessity, a MAP and a COMPASS.

The OS Lake District Tourist Map has been used throughout in preparing this book; I prefer it to OS 1:50,000 Nos. 89 and 90 which also cover the area as it shows the whole of the National Park on the one map, obviating the danger of finding yourself with the wrong map in your rucksack when the crunch comes. The same applies to the four OS 1:25,000 maps of the Lake District, although if you are prepared to go to the expense of buying all four you might find them useful for studying in advance to plot an unfamiliar route. Try to carry a compass of reputable make which is easy to read, and if you are unfamiliar with the use of map and compass spend some time in advance practising with a local map near home. Never think that as a sketch map is provided you can do without an overall map of the area, because if you then stray into a part not covered by your sketch map you will be totally lost. This applies to any unfamiliar district away from habitation, and particularly to the high fells.

Much has been said of rain and bad weather, but most of you will be walking in pleasant summer weather under blue, sunny skies. Carry extra drinks on those days; you won't find a cafe round every corner, and there is very little natural water above 2,000 ft. Nor is there any shade once you are above the tree line, so take a cotton hat with a brim to protect your head and neck, don't wear shorts, however much you may be tempted to, and take a garment with long sleeves to protect your arms from sunburn. Don't be put off by all these warnings. Seventy per cent of the time the weather will be fine, but you will take home unhappy memories if you go unprepared for the odd wet or too-hot day. One thing you don't have to worry about on the fells is what you look like; everyone dresses for practicality and survival and the more experienced the walker the more curious his or her kit is likely to be.

The often-repeated term 'cairn' deserves explanation. In the Lake District a cairn is a pile of stones raised to mark a

8

route. You will soon learn to recognise them and be able to trace where the path goes; if you are in any doubt pause for a moment and look for the next cairn. Where a path is indistinct there is usually a cairn ahead on the skyline. Try to start your walk early in the day so as to be safely back before nightfall. The walks in this book are set on good paths in popular terrain, so you can expect to have company from time to time along the way. At the time of publication all footpaths used in these walks were designated as official footpaths or rights of way, but it should be borne in mind that diversion orders may be made from time to time.

Although every care has been taken in the preparation of this Guide, neither the Author nor the Publisher can accept responsibility for those who stray from the Rights of Way.

Finally, the Lake District Weather Service on Windermere 5151 gives a recorded weather message, changed every twenty-four hours, reporting conditions on the fells as noted by the National Park wardens. It isn't easy to get connected to this number between eight and nine o'clock in the morning as everyone else is ringing it too, so try ringing the previous evening when you will very likely get the same report and be connected straight away.

Enjoy your holiday. If you are about to set foot on the fells for the first time, I envy you.

Elizabeth Cull
May 1990

LOCATION MAP

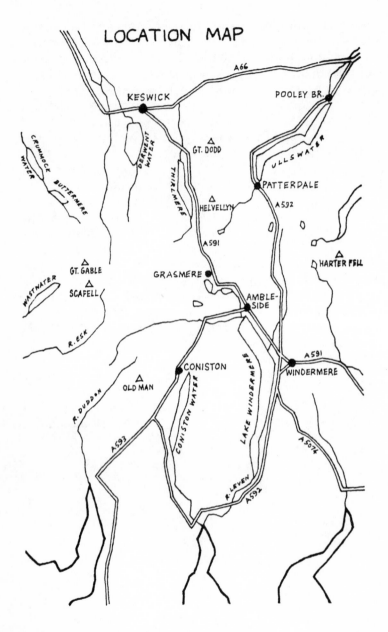

WALKS FROM GRASMERE

WALKS FROM GRASMERE

Gentle Grasmere, the very heart of Lakeland, set on the banks of the river Rothay, is the starting place for a variety of lovely walks. Grand walks to mountain tops – including Helvellyn – and little walks rising no more than eight or twelve-hundred feet. All are fell walks. Some, though, are short, such as that to tiny Alcock Tarn. Each follows a safe, well-defined path, and with the exception of the climb to Helvellyn, all are easily approached on foot from Grasmere village.

HELMCRAG
Distance – 3½ miles.
Approximate time – about 2 hours, there and back.

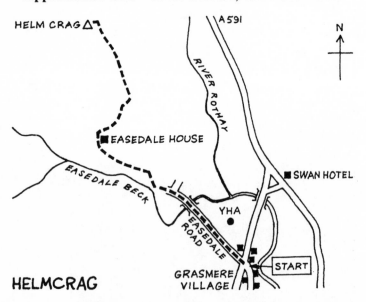

It is fair to say that this eminence rising 1,200 ft to the NW of Grasmere would be a less popular climb were it not for the famous 'Lion & Lamb' rocks that crown its summit, which are seen to such effect from the A591 road to Keswick. How fortunate, then, that these rocks exist to lure us to the top, since Helm Crag is an interesting mountain, with a mass of crag to explore on the summit.

The route up is simple and short; from the centre of Grasmere village it goes along Easedale Road to the famous Goody Bridge above Easedale Beck and, ignoring the fork where the road branches right, carries straight on until Easedale House is reached. Here it passes through a gate to cross the meadow towards a signpost pointing right to Helm Crag. Soon a second gate appears, where a signpost again indicates a right turn and the route follows the wall for a short distance until a path is seen leading to the top.

This makes a wonderful first walk for children. Neither too long nor too steep, yet it offers a challenge and gives a chance to examine at close quarters the famous rocks so plainly seen from below.

EASEDALE TARN
Distance – 4½ miles.
Approximate time – 3 hours, there and back.

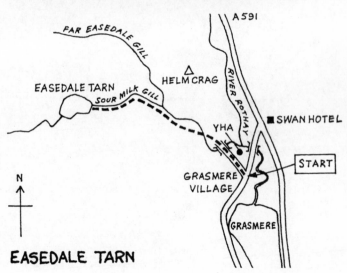

EASEDALE TARN

The route travels along Easedale Road for about half-a-mile until a sign is seen pointing left across a narrow bridge 'to Easedale Tarn'. The way crosses this bridge and another beyond it to go through a gate onto the bridle path where, after 500 yds and another gate, it is seen to cross a meadow. Two more gates, and the path turns upwards for about a mile beside the lovely foaming waterfalls of Sour Milk Gill, and the Tarn is reached.

Easedale Tarn lies in a great rocky basin with the mass of Tarn Crag above it; Sergeant Man is in the distance behind, and the Langdale Pikes away on the left.

The return to Grasmere is by the same route and arrival there completes a very pleasant four-mile walk. You will feel, rightly, that you have been into the heart of the fells, though at no point will the climb have exceeded 800 ft.

ALCOCK TARN
Distance – 2 miles.
Approximate Time – 1½ hours, there and back.

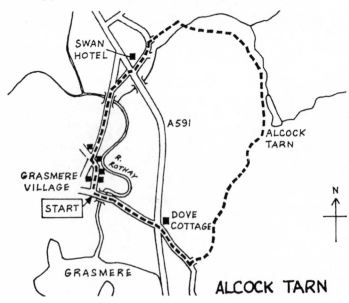

This little tarn, hardly more than a mile from the centre of Grasmere as the crow flies, is an easy destination for a hot summer day. It holds out the prospect of a swim and a laze on its grassy banks, and a visit to Wordsworth's *Dove Cottage* on the way.

The route leaves Grasmere at the southern end to cross the A591 and go off on the left to *Dove Cottage*. After passing the cottage it continues along the lane for about 500 yards to a track on the left sign-posted '*Alcock Tarn*'. This track runs straight on up the hill, then left over a bridge and through a gateway. On again, with rhododendrons flowering all around, when in season, and through an iron gate towards a little reservoir. It then passes a National Trust sign and soon afterwards reaches the tarn.

To return, either use the same path back to Grasmere, or make a circular tour by walking round to the far end of the tarn and following the footpath from there which bears left to come down alongside the beck at the back of the *Swan Hotel*.

GRISEDALE TARN, DOLLYWAGGON PIKE, and FAIRFIELD.
Distance from Grasmere to the Tarn – 4½ hours to the Tarn and back.

Brooding over Grasmere to the North-east are the heights of Dollywaggon Pike and Fairfield, both over 2,800 ft, and set in their valley is Grisedale Tarn. The following route is safe in misty weather, certainly as far as the tarn, and the gentle ascent by Tongue Gill makes it one of the easiest of fell walks. Only at the end is there anything approaching a scramble, yet one is cradled in hills all the way. Far from the road or any habitation, the silence is a pleasure broken only by the occasional bleating of Herdwicks, the trill of skylarks and the burble of the beck as it hurries down to join the river Rothay.

Here, one cold April day, I saw a fox, master of the fells as he loped between the boulders on Fairfield's grassy

15

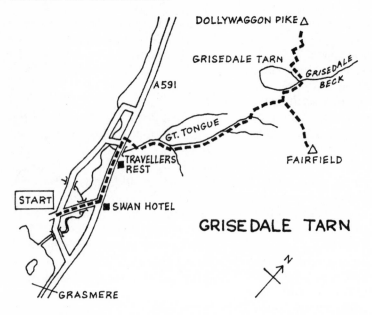

flanks. You might not be lucky enough to see him, but you will certaintly see moss campion and other alpines on Dolly-waggon, butterwort by the tarn, and the little yellow tormentil scattered everywhere from June to September.

The route leaves Grasmere at the northern end, to pass the *Swan Hotel* and follow the road towards Keswick to a group of houses just past the *Traveller's Rest* called *Tongue Ghyll Cottages*, where a footpath marked 'Helvellyn & Patterdale' passes in front of the cottages and leads to a gate at the top of the lane. On uphill it goes, keeping company with Tongue Gill splashing down on the right, for about ten minutes, when it goes through another gate onto the open fellside. Here the beck splits in two, with the wedge at Great Tongue separating Tongue Gill on the right from Little Tongue Gill on the left.

Crossing two bridges and passing a small caged reservoir, the way now bears left to follow the path above Tongue Gill and keeps beside the beck, climbing gradually all the time, for the best part of an hour. Then the path begins to slope away from the river and is cairned to rise sharply over a shattered, rocky mound. Thereafter, cairns appear frequently, every fifty yards or so, taking the path on past a boulder-strewn gulley by a waterfall and up a sharp scramble to an easy path across a plateau. Here care must be taken not to lose the path; the temptation is to stray into the scree and loose boulder on the left, so keep well to the right and look out for the big cairn in the distance at the head of the path. Beyond this cairn is Grisedale Tarn.

It takes about 2½ hours to reach the tarn from Grasmere village and about 2 hours to return the same way. Look around, however, beyond Grisedale Tarn to the North is Dollywaggon Pike with a clear zig-zag path leading to the summit. To the right of the tarn is a broad, grey boulder-and-scree path to Fairfield. If the weather is clear, to walk up Dollywaggon or scramble up Fairfield would turn a gentle amble into a quite creditable fell walk, with the added reward of superb views from either summit.

My own favourite is Fairfield. Though the ascent from the tarn is hard, once at the top a very fair field indeed will be found; a broad, grassy plateau leading to a long, undulating four-mile ridge walk which ends above Rydal Water. The view from the top reveals the whole Grisedale valley to Patterdale, with Eagle Crag, Helvellyn and Striding Edge on the left and to the right Deepdale and the black mass of St Sunday Crag, where grass of parnassus grows. When descending to Grisedale Tarn again you will find the going slightly easier by the big boulders of the broken wall on the left.

As an alternative to the Fairfield walk, the Dollywaggon zigzag is a longer but easier ascent. At the top the view is North across the crags of Nethermost Cove towards the summit of Helvellyn, or West across Birk Side and Comb Crags to peaceful Thirlmere nestling in its dark pines. Returning to Grisedale Tarn one takes in a view of the whole length of Deepdale Hause and St Sunday Crag rising above the valley. Then there is the quiet walk back to Grasmere along the grassy river bank beside the splashing water.

17

HELVELLYN
Distance to the summit and back – 4 miles.
Time – 4–5 hours, there and back.

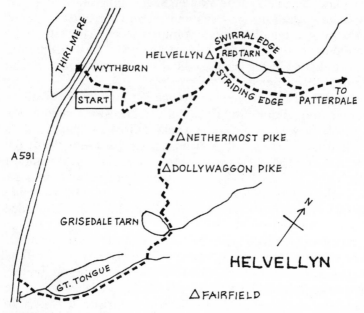

There are many routes to Helvellyn; one might start from
Threlkeld, Wythburn, Dunmail, Rydal, Deepdale or Glenridding, and though the approaches from the Grasmere side
lack the glamour of the climb from Glenridding, where
every step up the deep valley towards the menacing dark
peaks ahead is an excitement, they at least give one a
startlingly spectacular view of Striding Edge. Seen in swirl-
ing mist from the long saddle below the summit this stark
slice of black rock is thrilling beyond belief, though when
you finally reach the summit and stroll across to view it again
swinging down to meet its opposite number, the Swirral
Edge, at Red Tarn, it looks deceptively easy and inviting.
Before you decide, as most of us do, that you've just got to
walk those paths, think of the grim view you had from the
saddle and reflect that, easy though it looks from here, it is
still the same arrete!

The easiest and most direct route to the summit is from Wythburn, some four miles from Grasmere on the Keswick road, where Comb Gill runs into Thirlmere. There is a good car park, located by a telephone at the entrance, but it gets quite congested during the summer, and it might be a good idea to use the Ambleside–Keswick bus, which stops at Wythburn.

The delight of this route is that it starts climbing straight away. There is no disheartening trudge along a stony approach before you can get going, from the very first you know you are climbing a mountain and for the whole of the 3,116 ft to the summit every step is a step upwards.

As it leaves the shelter of the trees the path splits, and will do so several times more along the way. The little byeways are all part of the main route, having been formed where people have chosen to take a slightly longer way round to avoid a difficult bit. On the whole they are more useful when descending, though there is one little diversion just before the path leaves the shelter of the trees which neatly avoids a steep little rise over slippery rocks.

The route follows the path up the hillside, working round from east to north, till it comes to the one level stretch in the whole climb, the broad saddle below the summit. Here the ground falls away on both sides, to Thirlmere on the left and to Nethermost Cove on the right, and it is towards the edge above Nethermost that Striding Edge is seen to such advantage. Keep to the path, as there is no approach to Striding Edge until you reach the summit. In no time you will be there, and you can sit in a sheltered angle in the great summit cross, with your sandwiches and coffee.

If the day is fine enough to tempt you onto Striding Edge, walk across to the Eastern edge of the summit plateau where you will see the two ridges descending above the corries to meet in the middle at Red Tarn. The thing to do is to go down on the left by the Swirral Edge and return by Striding Edge on the right, cooling your feet in the tarn on the way. Put like that it sounds easy, but it will take at least two hours, and you will still have the descent to Wythburn to tackle afterwards.

There are only two possible pitfalls on the descent to Wythburn. The first comes at the outset; **care must be taken**, especially in mist, that starting from the shelter cross the path on the right of the cairn ahead is followed, as the path on the left leads to Striding Edge. The second hazard comes where the path splits just beyond the saddle into two routes of equal importance; the right-hand path is the route down to Wythburn, that on the left leading to Nethermost Cove and Dollywaggon Pike.

The canter down to Wythburn will take about an hour-and-a-half, and is great fun. On the way are lovely views over peaceful, pine-clad Thirlmere towards the Langdale Pikes on the left, the waterfalls, centre, splashing down from Greenup, and Blea Tarn further round to the right with the great mountains of Borrowdale rising behind. Ravens soar silently above, and with luck you will have left any fierce winds and stinging rain behind on the higher slopes and be galloping along in sunshine. Whether you choose to tackle Striding Edge or not, you will have had a day to remember!

If you prefer a gentler descent and have time to spare, the descent to Grisedale Tarn is recommended. For this you take the left-hand path at the saddle for Nethermost Cove and Dollywaggon Pike as mentioned above. This route brings you round Nethermost to the zig-zags on Dollywaggon and thence to Grisedale Tarn, to return to Grasmere beside Tongue Gill as described in the Grisedale Tarn walk. It is better not to attempt this descent unless the weather is fine.

This route descends to the road at Broadrayne, only half-a-mile from Grasmere but three miles from the car park at Wythburn, so is recommended for those going from Grasmere to Wythburn by bus.

Times: 2–2½ hours to the summit from Wythburn; about 2½ hours for the 'edges'; 1½ hours down to Wythburn from the summit; about 2½ hours to descend to Broadrayne. No refreshments except those you carry with you.

WALKS IN THE LANGDALES

WALKS IN THE LANGDALES

The high passes of Wrynose and Hard Knott which carry the road from the Langdales to the remote villages of Boot, Ulpha and Eskdale Green traverse some of the loneliest mountains in Lakeland. Even grim Honister does not cross such isolated country, and the road over Kirkstone Pass, for all its notoriety, is civilised in contrast.

At Hard Knott the way is a narrow, twisty, one-in-three track that snakes sharply up the fellside in a series of hair-raising curves. Wrynose is better only by comparison. But the country they span is unsurpassed for wild beauty, and if you are there during a fairly wet summer you will see the fell sides running with white water where dozens of tiny stream-lets foam down to meet the River Duddon. The area is lovely beyond belief, and yellow bog asphodel along the river bank adds greatly to its charm.

Watch out for the resident fell pony who stands in the middle of the road at Cockley Beck bridge waiting for hand-outs. Should you unwisely stop the car to give him a biscuit or an apple you'll be there all day!

At the bridge a road goes off on the left to Ulpha and Dunnerdale, but we bear right over the bridge for Hard Knott Pass, and soon the way becomes softer and greener as it runs through Eskdale. This is the territory of 'L'aal Ratty', the 15″ gauge Ravenglass and Eskdale railway that starts on the coast at Ravenglass and terminates at Dalegarth station, half-a-mile from Boot. For all children between nine and ninety a ride behind this little puffer is a 'must', and since there is a good car park at Dalegarth station it is simple to combine the ride with a walk on the gentle fells above Eskdale. The two walks which follow both start at Dalegarth and finish at Eskdale Green for a return ride on 'Ratty'.

RIVER ESK and STANLEY FORCE
Distance – 3 miles.
Time – about 1¼ hours.

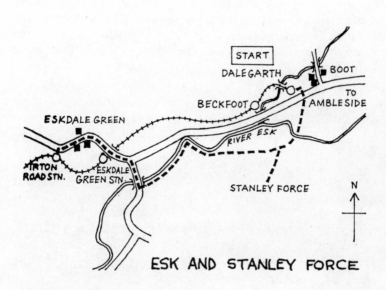

ESK AND STANLEY FORCE

From Dalegarth station turn left onto the road and walk a hundred yards or so to enter a little track on the right opposite Brook House. Walk along here to cross the River Esk beside the church, and continue for a very short distance to meet the footpath from Hard Knott.

Turn right onto this path, and when it comes close to the river again an obvious way will be seen going sharp left. This track leads through a little wood for a view of Stanley Force, at the foot of Birker Beck, a diversion which, though it adds half-a-mile to the walk, is recommended.

Soon after returning to the original path, a view of Dalegarth Hall will be seen on the right, before the way enters Low Wood. On leaving this wood the river bank is met again; stay beside the river, ignoring a path going off left at

23

Red Brow, until the Ulpha Road is reached at Forge Bridge. Here the path turns right to cross the river and follow the road for half-a-mile or so to Eskdale Green.

There are two stopping places for the train; Eskdale Green station just this side of the village and Irton Road, some half-a-mile beyond it. You would be sorry to miss Eskdale Green, which is a village of character, so continue through the village and join the train a little further on at Irton Road.

BECKFOOT TO BLEA TARN
Distance – 2½ miles.
Time – 1½ hours.

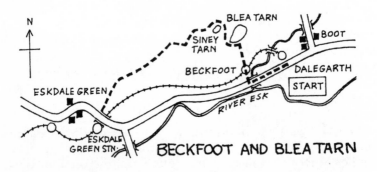

BECKFOOT AND BLEA TARN

This route climbs the fells behind Beckfoot Halt and visits Blea Tarn and Siney Tarn before descending at Eskdale Green almost opposite the railway station.

Unless you plan to ride the one stop from Dalegarth to Beckfoot, leave Dalegarth car park and turn right to walk half-a-mile along the road to Beckfoot Halt, where the route crosses the railway line to go through a five-barred gate onto the fell, and after following a wall for a few yards goes straight ahead up the hillside.

24

This uphill path bears slightly left (NW) for a twenty-minute climb to Blea Tarn. The route keeps to the broad, green path, avoiding two or three sheep tracks which wander off on the left and a little path that bears off right, until after a scramble up a ten-foot craggy knoll it bears left for the tarn.

Blea Tarn's grassy banks invite a halt, even a swim if the sun is hot enough, and there is time to relax here as the rest of the walk shouldn't take much more than an hour. This is the best spot for a picnic, the banks of Siney Tarn being far too boggy.

The route now circles Blea Tarn to the left to pick up a path going west to Siney Tarn, no more than ten minutes away. Although referred to as a tarn this is really a group of ponds, reedy and boggy, a lonely upland haunt for wild ducks. It is easy to lose the path on such soggy ground, but this is a fairly popular walk and the bootmarks of others will be a guide. The path goes right round Siney Tarn in a big circle to become a rather indistinct track over rising ground, slightly south-west. If you find yourself walking downhill in a north-westerly direction you have not made far enough round the tarns to pick up the correct path, which goes over a series of small humps until, within fifteen minutes of leaving the tarns, a really sizeable cairn is seen.

Look west from this cairn to a wall and fence in the middle distance, and you will see the path going diagonally to meet it. The path then follows this wall for a little way to a stile over a fence at right angles. Once over this stile, ignore the path which continues by the wall, and instead make straight ahead through the bracken on a narrow track crossing the fell towards a gateway.

Through this gate is a green path which runs downhill until a right turn through a pair of gates gives onto a stony track leading to the road. Turn right again on reaching the road and cross over for Eskdale Green halt.

Both these walks finish in style with a ride back on L'aal Ratty to Dalegarth Station and car park.

PIKE O'BLISCO from THREE SHIRE STONE
Distance – 3½ miles.
Time – About 2½ hours, in all.

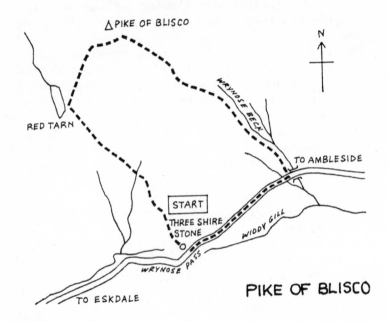

PIKE OF BLISCO

At the top of Wrynose Pass is the Three Shire Stone, marking the meeting place of the old counties of Cumberland, Westmorland and Lancashire. It would be a pity if any zealot in the cause of county reorganization sought to remove this stone as, apart from its historic interest, it marks the starting point of a fine short route to the 2,300 ft summit of Pike O' Blisco, a mountain every bit as lively as its name suggests.

There are plenty of places near the Stone where a car can be parked for the time it takes to climb to the great summit cairn and return, carrying back a memory of superb views from the top. All of Great Langdale can be seen, with Bowfell and Crinkle Crags close by on the left, Skiddaw far away to the north, Helvellyn and the High Street range in the distance to the east, and behind, nearer at hand, Coniston Old Man and Harter Fell.

The ascent commences in a north-westerly direction from the Three Shire Stone to pass on the right of Red Tarn where a clear path, marked by cairns, is seen leading to the summit. Either descend by the same route, or move around a little to the right of the cairn and pick up the path which goes down to join the road beside Wrynose Beck. A right turn onto the road there gives a half-mile walk back to the Three Shire Stone.

ESK FALLS and LINCOVE BECK
Distance – About 3 miles.
Time – There and back, 1½ hours.

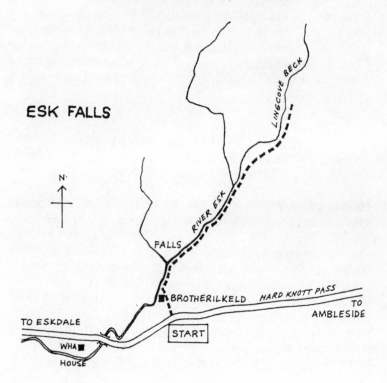

At Hard Knott Pass it is possible to look along the whole length of Eskdale to the sea. Nearer at hand is the old Roman Fort, and a little way past the fort a telephone by the road marks the start of a path on the right to Brotherilkeld Farm and the River Esk. Pass through the farmyard to pick up a track on the nearside bank of the river. The path runs well above the river at first, but later comes closer to it as the weight of rushing water cuts deep into the fellside towards the gorge of Esk Falls.

About two miles from Brotherilkeld the route crosses the famous packhorse bridge over Lincove Beck to the grassy banks of the river Esk, to view the magnificent Falls. This is the high point of the walk, and although it is possible to extend the walk by turning left after re-crossing the packhorse bridge to walk for a little way beside Lincove Beck, there is no alternative but to return to Brotherilkeld the way you came. Thre is a path on the right from Lincove Beck half-a-mile or so from the falls which returns to the road at Cockley Beck bridge, but this gives a tiring two-mile tramp along the road over Hard Knott Pass to reach Brotherilkeld again.

STICKLE GHYLL and PAVEY ARK
Distance – Short walk, 2 miles. Longer walk, 4½ miles.
Time – 1½ hours, 3½ hours.

How to get there: By bus from Ambleside to New Dungeon Ghyll Hotel, or by car via Skelwith Bridge and Elterwater.

One of the most spectacular short walks in Lakeland is that which climbs beside the thundering waterfalls of Stickle Ghyll to the magnificent hanging valley of Pavey Ark. No words of mine can adequately describe the exhilarating crash and thunder of the water, nor the thrilling first glimpse of that sheer, stark face rearing vertically beyond Stickle Tarn to a height of over 2,000 ft.

The popular route takes the path on the right bank of the

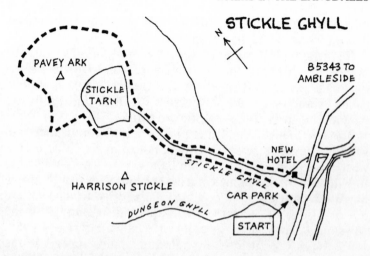

Ghyll, which is reached through a wooden gate at the back of New Dungeon Ghyll Hotel. Tramp upwards by the Ghyll for an hour or so until Stickle Tarn is reached, when the great black curtain of Pavey Ark will be seen rising on the far side.

You will never be lonely on this walk; hundreds travel the same ground every summer, but this only proves it is a walk not to be missed.

For most walkers the grimly splendid view and exciting walk by the waterfalls will be enough, but some will long to be up there on top of the Ark looking down, and why not? There is a walker's route known as Jack's Rake which rises from the foot of the Ark to cross the face from east to west, but inexperienced walkers have been warned off this route by the Lake District Wardens because of the poor condition of the path. An easier and safer way is to take the path to the west of the tarn towards Harrison Stickle, which means walking up to the tarn on the left bank of Stickle Ghyll. A path well to the left of the hotel which climbs a rise to a five-barred gate brings one to this left bank. Well away from the water at its start, it continues over a stile to breast another

29

rise, when it discloses a wonderful view of the falls roaring down close at hand on the right.

Now the path moves in beside the waterfall. The cascade booms down filling the air with spray and with a heady, ozone freshness, and on windy days the rocky path is washed clean by the water dashing across it. Once these falls are passed one soon comes to Stickle Tarn.

The route skirts the tarn to pick up a rather indistinct path slanting upwards towards a depression in the hills to the west. This path is cairned from half-way up where the route to Harrison Stickle comes in from the left. Towards the top a narrower path goes off right at a large cairn to lead up the massive ridge of the Ark. This path, too, is cairned all the way, but keep well to the right after passing a boggy patch when a series of buttressing walls and a fence appear, or the summit will be missed and instead a rocky path around the back of the Ark will lead too quickly down again to the tarn.

It is fortunate that Pavey Ark's summit cairn is well back from the edge, as there is a sheer drop down that forbidding face! As it is, there are spots where the path runs close to the drop, and the wind that seems always to whirl and tear round the summit is a hazard; it plucks and thrusts hither and thither, and prudence bids one **keep close into the rocks at one's back**. But the view is breath-taking. All that busy, rushing water, now so far below, is silent and still; cars in the car park are like a boxful of children's bricks, and the people climbing beside the river and drifting around the tarn are no more than coloured specks on the patchwork landscape. Below, too, are the villages of Elterwater and Little Langdale, and at least five separate stretches of water can be seen before the fells ripple away towards Lake Windermere.

Just below the summit is a plateau which makes an excellent sheltered spot in which to picnic.

The return to the tarn is quick and easy. Retrace your steps from the summit to the rocky walls at its base and turn right onto the cairned, easterly path around the back of the Ark. This leads to a rough, stony track going steeply down on which you should continue, ignoring all side paths, until the valley floor is reached. Here Stickle Ghyll is crossed by stepping stones to circle the tarn on its eastern bank and return past the waterfalls to New Dungeon Ghyll Hotel.

SKELWITH BRIDGE, LITTLE LANGDALE and ELTERWATER
Distance – 5½–6 miles, level walking.

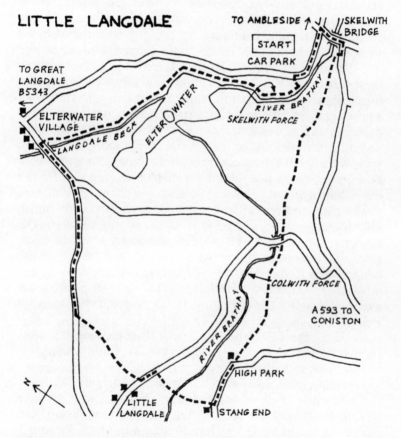

This fine circular route is pleasant walking all the way, almost all on level ground, and visiting the lovely falls of

31

Skelwith and Colwith Force. Halfway round at Little Langdale a good bar lunch is available, and other refreshments can be found at Elterwater and Skelwith Bridge. The 516 Ambleside to Dungeon Ghyll bus stops at Skelwith Bridge, or a car can be left in the National Trust car park, about 500 yds up the Elterwater road from the Bridge.

The route bears left from this car park, and after following the road for a short distance goes through a gap in the wall on the right for the footpath to Skelwith Force. After wandering off to bridges and vantage points above the seething waters, it continues by the riverside through the yard of the Kirkstone Green Slate Quarries to come out onto the road at Skelwith Bridge. Here it turns right to cross the bridge over the River Brathay, and almost immediately turns right again for a few yards along the Coniston road where, ignoring the footpath marked 'Skelwith Force only', it passes the Rosewood Tea Gardens and goes through a kissing gate onto the path for Colwith Bridge.

Now the path meanders through the trees to a grassy field at the top, where it is joined by another coming in from the left. The single path now continues towards the distant hills.

Through another kissing gate the path bears left until, after passing some cottages, it seems to disappear in the corner of a field. In fact it crosses the wall by a narrow stone stile and travels at right-angles through the centre of the hedge behind the cottages. Emerging, it crosses another meadow and stile to a downhill path by the river, coming out eventually onto the roadway a few steps from Colwith Bridge.

Crossing the road, the route now travels along the footpath opposite signposted *'High Park & Little Langdale'*, which leads to Colwith Force.

Fortunately more remote from the road than Skelwith, Colwith Force is like a grotto hidden in trees, with solitude adding to its quiet beauty. When the Force is passed, the path goes on for some way beside the river before leaving it to go uphill for a short distance to a little clearing where, by a National Trust sign, it bears away left. Leave the path here, and go instead through the five-barred gate opposite, keeping by the wall for some fifty yards to go through a gap and down right towards the few houses of High Park.

At High Park the way turns right to follow the road for about a quarter of a mile, then right again onto the sign-posted footpath to Little Langdale.

This sheltered, grassy path runs downhill across two fields to turn left by a white-painted bungalow towards the village of Little Langdale, not two hundred yards away. Here at the *Three Shires Inn* you will find a friendly welcome and good bar snacks, but on your way to the inn do not fail to mark the path on to Elterwater, which goes off right between two cottages, through a five-barred gate, and across a meadow, to turn right again onto a stony path. At yet another five-barred gate it ignores the little path going left uphill and keeps to the stony track for about half-a-mile, to join a narrow roadway and turn first right then left for Elterwater village.

For the return to Skelwith Bridge, cross Great Langdale Beck at Elterwater bridge and turn sharp right across the car park and through a kissing gate onto the path along the river bank.

Thus this pleasant walk ends with a gentle amble by a river whose summer banks show pink campion, forget-me-not and yellow buttercup, with vetches climbing among the wild roses and blackberry blooms. On goes the way by the soft-flowing waters and quiet meres until, most unexpectedly, the roar and rush of Skelwith Force is met again half-a-mile downstream, and another walk is over.

WALKS FROM BUTTERMERE

WALKS FROM BUTTERMERE

Buttermere village, whether you drive to it over steep, spectacular Honister Pass with its near-vertical slaty sides sweeping down to the road's very edge, or through green, bird-haunted Newlands, is a good centre for walks. There is parking space, but as the car parks get very full in high summer an alternative is to to use the regular bus service or the Mountain Goat minibus from Keswick. Times of departure can be obtained from the information centre in Keswick Moot Hall.

The Lake District Tourist Board has kindly sign-posted various walks: around the lake, alongside Crummock Water, the climb to Scale Force, and a short, pretty walk through the National Trust property of Ghyll Wood, its way through the trees beside the rushing waters of Sail Beck cushioned with tormentil. Enter by the kissing-gate opposite Bridge Hotel carpark for this pleasant half-hour's wander in the sun-dappled shade.

For a real fell walk though, try this one to Bleaberry Tarn and on to the summit of Red Pike, returning to Buttermere via Scale Force. It is a stiff climb to the summit, but once there all the world is laid out before you with magnificent views in every direction, and on a clear day you can see Scotland and the Isle of Man. **Do not confuse our Buttermere Red Pike with Wasdale Red Pike over on the other side of Ennerdale, beyond Pillar.**

BLEABERRY TARN, RED PIKE, HIGH STILE
Distance – 4½–6 miles, hard walking.

Start this walk on the path signposted 'Scale Force', to the left of the *Fish Hotel*. After a few minutes the Scale Force route goes through a wooden gate, and here you leave it to pass instead through the iron gate on your left. Carry on over a stile to skirt the lake and cross two wooden bridges,

36

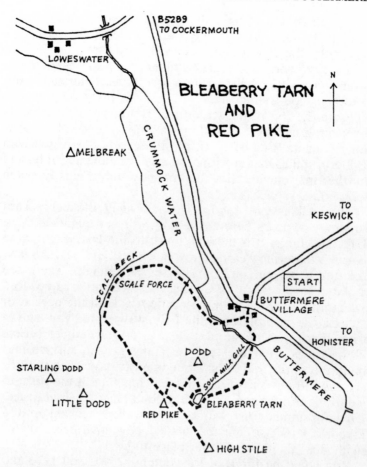

then go through a kissing-gate to the 'Path Round the Lake'. Cross over this path and strike up the bank opposite onto yet another path which you also cross, to take a not very obvious track up through the trees ahead marked by a large cairn at its foot.

This stony path leads you up through the trees for half-an-hour, to climb a flimsy stile over a wire fence before continuing across the open fellside. Here on a hot day walking in the shade of trees is a delight, but an application of anti-midge cream might make the day pleasanter. Once over the stile at the top a great stone 'staircase' leads to a red scree scramble; the ascent there seems slightly easier on the left, and in late spring or early summer the voice of a cuckoo from across the valley calls a wry commentary on your efforts as you toil upwards.

From the top of the scree there is an easy, cairned walk over the green fellside to the tarn. Now you see the reason for the name 'Bleaberry Tarn'; the fellside is covered with Bilberry spikes, heavy with berries in late June and July, and by the time one reaches the tarn lips and fingers are blue with bilberry juice.

The walk is hard, and it is a joy when Bleaberry Tarn suddenly appears before you. As with so many of these Lakeland tarns, it is hidden almost to the last; one minute you're wondering wearily 'How much further?' and the next the tarn is before you, sparkling in the sunlight. The shore makes a lovely place for a picnic, cradled in the lap of Red Pike and High Stile with the gentle trickle of the beck over its bed, the rush of Sour Milk Gill away behind you, and in front the waters of the tarn clear as crystal, until a breeze blows down from the tops sweeping up the surface into hundreds of tiny wavelets. Even on misty days when the hills are snuffed out and all but the first few feet of the path up Red Pike is obliterated, this is a good place to sit at peace. On a hot summer day, with cheerful walkers tacking up Red Pike in a steady stream and the lake edge invitingly cool for swimmers, there is no better place to be.

You could be forgiven for contenting yourself here and lazily returning to Buttermere the way you came, were it not for the marvellous view waiting for you at the top of the Pike and the achievement of scrambling up it. And in truth, though the route to the top looks scarifying from the tarn it is certainly no more difficult, and in some ways easier, than the path up from Buttermere.

The way up Red Pike is that red scree scramble you see over to the right (W) of the tarn. As you begin your climb up from the tarn the rounded, heather-covered slopes of Dodd lie slightly behind to the right, and not until you attain a good height does Dodd fade into insignificance and Buttermere village come into view beyond it. As suddenly as you came upon Bleaberry Tarn so will you reach the peak of Red Pike; you toil over yet another mound, and there is the summit cairn before you and all around you breath-taking views; Buttermere village nestling between its twin lakes of Buttermere and Crummock Water with Robinson's, Dale Head and the Buttermere Fells rising behind. Come round right to the black cleft of Honister Pass, Fleetwith Pike on the right above, High Stile and Chapel Crags immediately before you and Scafell to the right of them away in the distance (Gable is hidden), then Pillar, Scoat Fell and Steeple above Ennerdale's wooded sides and away beyond Ennerdale Water the plumed chimneys of Calder Hall. On a really clear day you should then see the sea and the Isle of Man, but local lore decrees that if you do it will rain next day. Don't worry, it will probably rain next day anyway!

Next to the right and nearer at hand is Loweswater, then in the distance again the Solway Firth and the dim hills of Scotland – one of them is Criffel – round to Crummock Water and Buttermere again, with a tiny scrap of Derwentwater, Skiddaw and Blencathra behind. Overhead the scudding clouds pattern it all, now light, now dark, and you may even hear the cry of trail hounds calling from across the valley. Yes, up here on a fine day one is heir to the kingdom, and it would be an insensitive walker indeed who failed to pause for a long, long look at it all before pushing on to Scale Force or going back down to the tarn.

At first the path to Scale Force is not at all clear, but point yourself towards Ennerdale Water and you will see the first of the cairns. Once locate this cairn and you'll be down the slither and onto the green plateau below in no time, and then it's just a question of following the landmarks. **If it is misty and you are unable to locate the landmarks described, particularly the lakes, you should not attempt the Scale Force route but return to Buttermere via the tarn and the known path.**

On the descent to Scale Force there is a clear path to the extreme right; ignore this and steer a middle course roughly across the plateau mid-way between the fence on the left and the right-hand edge. You lose Ennerdale Lake as you go, but Loweswater is visible ahead and Crummock Water down on the right with the wedge of Mellbreak rising between them. Make dead centre for Mellbreak and as the two lakes recede and Mellbreak becomes more prominent you will strike a pair of cairns guarding a red pathway which winds downhill to the left. Turn onto this rocky red path for Scale Force, which you can probably hear already roaring away down its steep, rocky chasm. Soon the head waters of Scale Beck begin to gather on the left, and the path turns to follow the beck as it flows ever faster towards the waterfall. Deeper and deeper the beck cuts into its cleft, and as it deepens, choose your time to move over to the edge for your view of Scale Force. There is a single wooden plank where the beck starts to run into calmer water which makes an excellent viewpoint if you're brave enough to cross it.

Soon after you pass this plank the path is cairned away from the beck uphill to the right. This is your route back to Buttermere; try not to miss it because if you follow the beck too far down you'll find yourself trudging across the soggy waste that borders Crummock Water, and add at least half an hour to your walk. It should take you about an hour and a half to climb up to the tarn from Buttermere; about three hours to go on to the summit of Red Pike from the tarn and back to Buttermere via Scale Force, or about two and a half hours to go up Red Pike and back via the tarn to Buttermere.

There is a quicker, more direct route for the agile up from Buttermere to the tarn, by Sour Milk Gill. For this route you ignore the cairned track through the wood from the lakeside, and instead, after crossing the two wooden bridges you turn right to climb a sturdy ladder stile over the wall at the foot of Sour Milk Gill and pick your way up on its banks. This will bring you eventually to the tarn, missing out the 'staircase' and the red scree scramble. **It is important to cross the gill onto the left-hand bank when you can, if you neglect to do so you'll be hauling yourself up by the heather over the rise on the right in a most foolhardy fashion!**

WALKS AROUND HIGH STREET

WALKS AROUND HIGH STREET

Across the eastern fells between Windermere and Penrith runs the old Roman road known as High Street, the longest continuous footpath in Lakeland. This group of six walks is centred on the High Street range, around Martindale, Mardale and Kentmere.

Walking here in early spring one sees great swathes of Wordsworth's little dancing daffodils, the lenten lilies, while on the fells above them all is still winter and fingers of snow sparkle over the black rocks like frozen waterfalls. Birdseye primrose grows at Mardale, and one summer I saw a marsh gentian in a soggy spot near Blea Water, while in autumn the thrilling roar of rutting stags booms above Ullswater.

The land around Haweswater was flooded in 1929 to make a reservoir, drowning the tiny village of Mardale beneath its waters. Yet occasionally, when rainfall is exceptionally low, the level of Haweswater falls enough for the pathetic outlines of the eighteenth-century church, the cottages and the Dun Bull Inn to be visible in their watery grave.

The walk to Small Water is perfect; short and easy, it keeps company with the roistering beck for most of the way and passes within touching distance of two waterfalls. The other short walk, to Blea Water, is not so fine but it leads on to an exciting ridge walk on Riggindale Crags where the Lakeland Eagles nest. As good a walk as you will find anywhere.

For the start of these walks make for Bampton, either leaving the M6 at Shap or taking the road to 'Askham and Bampton' at Pooley Bridge. If the latter, you will pass on the way the Lowther Wild Life Park which is well worth a visit. Make for Haweswater from Bampton, driving along the lakeside to the car park at the road's end.

SMALL WATER and HARTER FELL
Distance – Short walk, 2 miles. Long walk, 5½–6 miles.
Times – Short walk, under 1 hour. Long walk, 2½ hours.

Route: To the right of the five-barred gate that leads from the car park a signpost marks three paths – to Kentmere, Bampton, and Longsleddale. The Small Water walk takes the broad, rutted centre path to Kentmere.

The path winds about a bit but it is easy to follow over the rocks and alongside the beck, climbing more steeply beside the waterfalls until it leaps the final grassy mound to reveal the tarn, almost at your feet.

It is indeed a 'small water', but very lovely, beautifully set in a tiny basin below the menacing grey mass of Harter Fell,

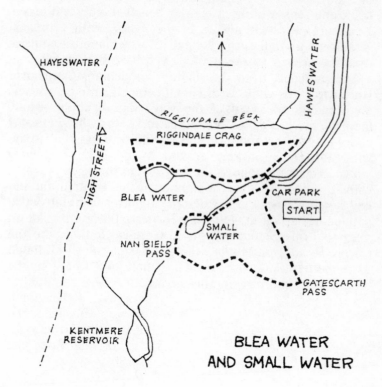

BLEA WATER
AND SMALL WATER

rocks forming a natural lip around its edge. The tarn makes a lovely spot for a picnic, and afterwards you can either return the way you came or go on to the longer walk over Harter for a look down into Kentmere and Long Sleddale.

Harter Fell (not to be confused with the other Harter Fell in Dunnerdale, far to the west) is seen at its best from Small Water. From the Kentmere side it is just a grassy hill, but here all is scree and boulder and grey rock, inaccessible but for the one path to Nan Bield Pass, the old pony track from Shap and Mardale to Kentmere and Windermere. The summit is 2,539 ft, and the distance from the tarn over Harter and back to Haweswater is 3½–4 miles.

The route goes round to the right of Small Water and then is cairned uphill to the great, square shelter cairn at the head of Nan Bield Pass. Looking down into Kentmere from this cairn one sees a different world, peaceful, soft and green. Kentmere reservoir nestles in the valley, with Froswick, Yoke and Ill Bell rising behind it, a tremendous contrast from the fierce rocks over which you have been toiling.

The path left from the shelter cairn climbs easily over Harter towards Gatescarth Pass, keeping Kentmere in view on the right for most of the way. Within about twenty minutes you are at the summit cairn, a surrealistic mass of oddly-angled fenceposts in the middle of a grassy plateau, with stonechats chirping around it and skylarks singing above. The route follows the fence from the cairn, keeping with it as it turns off at a right-angle, and within another half-hour it comes to the gate-opening where a well-trodden path comes up on the left from Haweswater and goes down right to Long Sleddale. This is Gatescarth Pass, the old Corpse Road from Mardale that leads eventually to Kendal. Take the left-hand path for an easy half-hour trot along the broad, down-hill path to Haweswater.

BLEA WATER and RIGGINDALE CRAG
Distance – Short walk, 3 miles. Long walk, 5 miles.
Times – Short walk 1½ hours. Long walk 2½ hours.

The way to Blea Water runs to the right beside the wall after passing through the five-barred gate, where the signpost points towards Bampton. After two hundred yards it goes down a set of wooden steps, crosses a small beck by stepping stones and on through a gap in another wall to cross Mardale Beck by a concrete slab bridge and turn sharp left to follow the beck. Though indistinct in places it continues beside the beck for about a mile, going through a gate where the beck gushes down a gorge and over a small dam beside the waterfall. Indeed, in places it is not one path but many, all making across the fell to the same destination – Blea Water.

This is the largest of the many tarns that dot the high land between Harter Fell and High Street and, again, makes a good spot for a family picnic. A short scramble up the grassy mound to the south-east will show you Small Water below, and you will have no difficulty in making across to it for the other route back to the car park.

For the longer walk over Riggindale Crag, follow the narrow path to the right of Blea Water for a hundred yards or so around the shore to a small cleft in the hillside where water runs, marked by a small cairn at its foot. A scramble up this cleft brings you onto a path striking diagonally up towards the ridge of the hill, where you turn right towards a small patch of water ahead. This small tarn lies at the commencement of the walk over Riggindale Crag, and crag it is indeed, as you will find.

Follow the path as it skirts the tarn to turn due east for two good miles of ridge walk before dropping steeply down to Haweswater, on the opposite bank from the car park. All the way along the ridge the views are superb; Blea Water and Small Water below lie leaden and sullen in dull weather, but when the sun shines they sparkle and glitter as though a myriad of silver fish sported in their translucent waters. Haweswater is on the left, getting gradually larger as you go

45

until the whole lake is in view, and on the left too are the grey scree slopes of Riggindale Fell with Riggindale Beck glinting down in the valley below. Over on the right are the crags of Long Stile and Dudderwick, with Harter's forbidding grey mass rising behind them.

It is wonderfully exhilarating up here on the high ridge. The wind sweeps across, the ground falls steeply away on either side, and somewhere on those slopes below the eagles nest. All too soon the path descends, leaving these glories behind. Keep to the zig-zag as you go, **and do not shorten the route by going straight down the hillside**.

As the path nears the bottom it seems to disappear over a grassy knoll and the temptation is to turn right to regain it, but in fact you should continue straight on when you will soon come to the path again. It then goes down, through bracken on the lower slopes, to join the Bampton path at a wall by the lakeside, where it turns right towards the car park.

KENTMERE and NAN BIELD PASS
Distance – Long walk to Pass, 8½ miles.
Short walk to Reservoir, 5 miles.
Times – Long walk, 4 hours. Short walk, 2 hours.

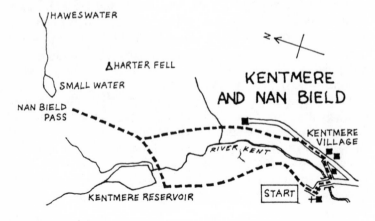

The leafy drive from Staveley to tiny Kentmere village is a joy, especially with the prospect of a good walk to add to the pleasure. Along the narrow lane winding past Fell Foot little tumbling waterfalls frolic beside the road, and the enclosing banks are gay with harebells, campion and Welsh poppies, but not until you reach the village do you catch more than a tantalising glimpse of the fells in their dark, craggy glory.

There is parking space near the church in Kentmere village, and from there the route follows the lane on the left of the church for about three hundred yards to go through the gate at Hartriggs Farm, where it follows the metalled track beside the beck for a mile or so then goes through another gate by signposts 'to Kentmere' and 'to Mardale'.

Following the Kentmere path, it climbs a little now towards the ring of fells that enclose the reservoir. Passing a farm on the right, it goes through the left-hand gate of a pair and continues under the shadow of Rainbarrow Crag on the left to go through yet another gate at Reservoir Cottage. Here the route bears left where the path forks, becoming less stony as it winds round the bracken-covered hillside towards the weirs below the reservoir where it crosses the River Kent by a plank bridge.

As you cross this bridge you can see the col of Nan Bield Pass in the hills ahead to the NNE, with the great shelter cairn standing square in the depression, though from here it seems no more than a hump against the horizon. After crossing the bridge, make sharply up the hillside gaining height rapidly to intercept the path to Nan Bield that traverses the hillside about 100 ft above the water. The climb is not arduous, and the summit of the Pass reveals a lovely view down to Haweswater.

Though not so spectacular as some of the more popular valleys, Kentmere has great charm. Butterwort and lousewort abound, and in high summer when cars are crawling through the Langdales in a steady stream and the slopes of Helvellyn are like rush hour on the underground, lonely, windswept Kentmere, its turf blue with devil's-bit scabious and spattered with yellow tormentil, is a haven of peace.

47

The route ends at the shelter cairn on Nan Bield, but before returning pass round the cairn and walk a hundred yards or so to the edge of the plateau to gaze upon Small Water in its tiny basin and Haweswater beyond, with Riggindale Crag rising above it. The path left from the cairn leads to a grand walk over Mardale Ill Bell to High Street, returning to Kentmere via Froswick and Ill Bell and the Garburn Pass. **(This is a long walk and you should not attempt it unless you have a good map and a compass and know how to use them).**

To vary the route back, return towards the bridge above the weirs but instead of descending the hill to cross it keep to the cairned track, which leads back by an interesting route to Kentmere village, ideal for those not averse to crossing becks by stepping stones!

Coming towards habitation, the route goes through an iron gate and thence to a farm, where it turns left through a wooden gate onto the road for a short distance, then through another wooden gate onto a bridleway. At the end of the bridleway it turns right to the road and keeps to it for half-a-mile. Soon Kentmere Church is seen in the valley below right; the route to it is along a lane leading steeply downhill beside a farm, just past a signpost pointing the bridle-path to Mardale.

Altogether this is a most pleasant, quiet walk, not difficult, and traversing country that varies from the lush Kentmere farmlands to the craggy heights of Harter, and with the drive to Kentmere village it makes a wonderful day out.

POOLEY BRIDGE and HOW TOWN,
returning by lake steamer
Distance – 5 miles.
Walking time – 2 hours, plus return by steamer.

This walk from Pooley Bridge to How Town, though lovely in fine weather, is a gift for days when the mist keeps one down below a thousand feet. It takes you in part along the

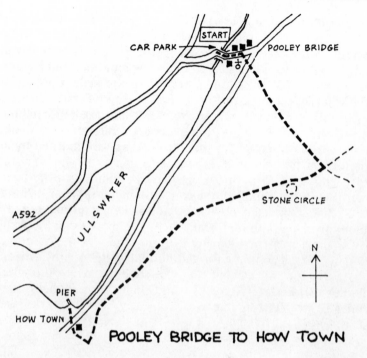

POOLEY BRIDGE TO HOW TOWN

Roman road, past a stone circle whose origin is a mystery, to come gradually down to the pretty village of How Town for a snack at the hotel before boarding the lake steamer to return to Pooley Bridge. On the way one has spectacular views of Ullswater, dark blue in the sunlight and watched over by brooding hills which seem to twist away at the far end into a black cavern. Pied Piper country, haunting and mysterious; some think it the most beautiful in all Lakeland.

The route starts at Pooley Bridge, passes the Sun Hotel and the shops to take the first turning on the right signposted 'How Town'. Here it continues over the crossroads where another signpost points to 'Roe Head', for rather more than half-a-mile, until the road ends at a farm. Then it goes through a gate onto the fell.

Now the broad, green pathway goes over the fell for

49

three-quarters of a mile to a large cairn marking its junction with the Roman road. It turns right here to follow High Street to the Stone Circle, not just a circle of stones but a fairy ring of close-cropped green fescue amid the rough grass and heather. By the Stone Circle the route bears right onto the track which crosses Barton Fell to How Town.

Soon the hills will rise on your left and the fell become more wild and desolate. After about a mile another small path crosses at an angle, the left-hand section marked by a pattern of flat stones which seem to mark the way; ignore this, and keep to the path you are on, coming shortly to a cairn set in the middle of the way. Still in the same direction, the route crosses a beck on stepping stones at a small gorge, then takes the path that bears right, keeping beside the wall for a short way then leaving it to go straight on SW, cross two becks and continue for another half-mile to How Town.

At the time of writing the lake steamer leaves the Pier Pooley Bridge at 12.05, 2.35 and 5.05, but do check the times before starting out.

WALKS IN BORROWDALE

WALKS IN BORROWDALE

AROUND STY HEAD

It is in the fastness of the fells that the best walks are found; if you take the bus from Keswick to Seatoller or drive round Derwentwater on the Borrowdale Road you will find yourself in a magical world of green hills with bright tumbling becks, rocky paths and scree scrambles. This is the country of the Sty, the old pack-horse road from Seathwaite to Wastwater.

Here are five walks around the Sty, and whether you choose the easiest walk to Sty Head Tarn, the highest over Thornythwaite and Glaramara, or the longest to Wasdale Head and back, you will go home knowing you have set foot in the very heart of the fells. You may see moss campion and purple saxifrage on the crags, the delicate, silver-edged leaves of alpine lady's mantle on the higher ranges, starry saxifrage in the clefts, and lousewort and butterwort everywhere. You will walk in the shadow of Scafell and Great Gable, and the splash and roar of Lakeland waters will be ever in your ears – a sound that will follow you home down the motorway to haunt your dreams till it lures you back again.

1. Simple route from Seathwaite to Sty Head,
following the pack-horse road.
Approximate distance – 6 miles from the farm and back.
Time – 3–3½ hours, from the farm and back.

From the bus stop at Seatoller, take the road signposted 'Seathwaite' and follow it for best part of a mile to the farm. There is ample parking space on the verge as the farm comes into view.

For this easy walk, ignore the marked footpath on the right between the farm buildings and continue instead

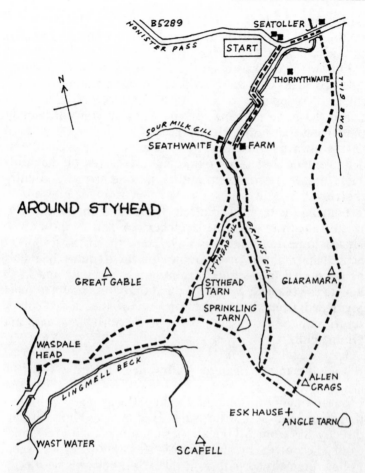

AROUND STYHEAD

straight on past the farm along the stony roadway that is part of the original pony track to Sty Head and Wastwater. When you reach the five-barred gate pass through it and continue along the path for another quarter of an hour to Stockley Beck Bridge. At the far end of the bridge is a gate, and after passing through it push on up the hillside ahead to yet another gate at the top of the rise.

You then strike diagonally with the path towards the clump of trees standing above Taylor Gill Force. Once there, you will find yourself looking down on the Force as it thunders through the cleft below, with a wonderful view of the scaly hillside beyond it.

Follow the path through the trees till it brings you alongside Sty Head Gill, which will keep you company almost to the tarn. When you come to a wooden footbridge, cross the gill to the opposite bank, or you will find yourself later on the wrong side of Sty Head Tarn.

It is always an excitement to reach a tarn; peaks are an achievement, but tarns mark out the stages of the walk. They suggest refreshment and invite one to rest and enjoy the view.

Leaving the tarn on your left, keep along the same south-westerly path towards the stretcher box and signpost at Sty Head, some ten minutes away. Here the paths go left to Scafell and right to Great Gable, **but these routes should not be attempted unless you have map and compass and know how to use them**. It will take you about 1½–2 hours to reach Sty Head from Seathwaite, and about the same time to return either by the same route or via Sprinkling Tarn and Grains Gill.

2. From Sty Head to Seathwaite, via Grains Gill

From the signpost, take the broad pathway marked 'Scafell' that runs south-east towards Esk Hause. Sprinkling Tarn lies directly SE from Sty Head Tarn, though they are hidden from each other by the rise of Seathwaite Fell between. Follow the cairned path as it takes you upwards beside the beck, and soon after the path crosses the beck you come to Sprinkling Tarn. This is a better place to rest and eat than Sty Head Tarn, which is the haunt of a nasty little biting black fly. Sit for ten minutes at Sty Head Tarn with the grandeur of Gable before you and Scafell rising at your back, and you'll be scratching for a fortnight!

Continue past Sprinkling Tarn, along the same path, and as you come over a slight rise, Grains Gill will be seen on the left with the red pathway alongside it that will take you north-east back to Stockley Beck bridge and the farm. To reach this path you must cross the beck by one of the sets of stepping stones, then follow close beside Grains Gill until it goes down into a cleft, when the path is cairned over the hillside a little to the right. After following the path for about half-an-hour you will see the farm and the road back to Seatoller in the valley below. As you come to the valley bottom, do not miss the gap in the wall on your left that takes you back over Stockley Beck Bridge to the farm, where a welcome cup of tea can be bought if the snack bar is open.

3. From Seathwaite to Sty Head, via Taylor Gill Force

Although at times more difficult, this route avoids the long drag up the stony track to Stockley Beck bridge. It is a more interesting route and the path around the hillside is narrow and steep, lending a touch of adventure to the walk.

At the farm, take the marked footpath between the farm buildings, cross the first footbridge, and ignoring the second bridge go through the wooden gate in the wall on your left to follow the footpath alongside the beck. The path runs beside the beck, cut off by the fence on the right, for about five minutes, then it leaves the water and strikes out over the hillside, still parallel with the beck but about thirty yards to the right of it. Make for a gap in the wall ahead, after which cairns guide you on across the hillside, still in the same direction. Soon you get a good view of Taylor Gill Force roaring down the hillside. The exciting closeness of rushing water makes this seem a far more spectacular sight than the long lacy falls of Sour Milk Gill which could be seen from the road on the way to the farm. Distance does not always lend enchantment to the view!

You can now see the lie of the path quite clearly as it goes on around the rocky hillside. Follow the cairns up a stony scramble, through a wooden gate and across a scree patch to pass by the top of the Force. Even on this rocky path grow the little Lakeland flowers, tormentil, starry saxifrage and butterwort, and it is heartening when the way grows narrow and steep and your face is crammed against the rock to find on a tiny ledge right before your eyes a little clump of pink heather or a butterwort.

It will take you an hour from the farm to reach the clump of fir trees above the waterfall. The swelling green fells opposite, rising to 2,500 ft, are Thornythwaite and Glaramara; if you find them enticing, turn to the last walk in this section where you will find described a route across their tops.

From the clump of trees above the waterfall a little pink path runs around the hillside, keeping close to Sty Head Beck, until it reaches the tarn. Then if you really want a good walk the most natural thing is to follow the path to the signpost as described in (1) and go on from there to Wasdale Head. If you start out from Seathwaite by ten o'clock you should make it comfortably to the bar of Wasdale Head Hotel, that legendary meeting place of climbers and fell walkers, to slake a royal thirst before it closes for the afternoon.

4. From Sty Head to Wasdale Head, and back.
Approximate Time – From the farm, and back, 5–6 hours.
Distance – 10 miles.

From Sty Head, the path to Wastwater goes to the right of the stretcher box towards the big cairn ahead, after which it skirts low down on Gable and Wasdale Fell before coming down to the valley for the last half-mile to the hotel. At the outset, this path is the only and obvious one going west past the big cairn, and is well marked all along its way above the beck. Rocky and barren, with hardly a trace of vegetation and no water save the tantalising silver thread of Lingmell Beck silent and still far down in the valley, it is a royal road, well trodden by the feet of the faithful. The grey bastions of Scafell and Scafell Pike loom from across the valley, and as you leave the deep heart of Cumbria behind you Wastwater comes into view ahead, decorated by tiny orange and yellow tents in the Forestry Commission's campsite at Wasdale Head.

It is possible to finish the walk at Wasdale Head and return by Mountain Goat 'Wasdale Flyer', which terminates at the hotel. The ride back to Ambleside over Hard Knott and Wrynose and on through the Langdales is incomparable, and from Ambleside you could get a bus back to Keswick. But if you intend to do this make enquiries first from Windermere 5161 or any Mountain Goat terminal about a seat on the Flyer.

To return on foot to Sty Head, start back by the path on which you came but where the path splits, instead of going back round the hillside take the right-hand fork to Lingmell Beck. Though a bit damp at times, this route makes very pleasant walking, especially on a hot day. The path follows quite close to the beck which bubbles along on the right at a great rate, tumbling over the rocks in a series of little waterfalls; the banks are dotted with flowers, everywhere is the aromatic perfume of bog myrtle, dippers and wagtails fly above the beck, and the whole thing is great fun after the rather dour walk of the morning.

You are making for that waterfall ahead where Lingmell Beck spurts over the top of the fell. As the water gouges deeper between the Rowan trees you'll find diminutive cairns taking you away towards the left so that you pass the waterfall almost without realising it and are walking once more upon a green path, still with the beck on your right. Finally the cairns take you well away to the left, leaving the beck behind for good, and within ten minutes you're back at Sty Head.

After your long walk you'll probably want to take the easy route home, so follow the Seathwaite path from the signpost back to the tarn and thence alongside Sty Head Beck until you come to the wooden footbridge. Here you cross over to the opposite bank to return to Seathwaite by Stockley Beck Bridge. **Do not neglect to cross the footbridge**, or you will find yourself at the end of a long day wearily attempting the difficult route home by Taylor Gill Force.

This walk to Wasdale Head and back is a long one, and you will need to reserve a full day for it. You won't go much above 1,700 ft, but if you start out by the more interesting route to the waterfall you will get a bit of a climb here, and the rocky Wastwater path is interesting. If you are not too tired, why not return from Sty Head by Grains Gill as described earlier, when you will come home in style!

5. High route over Thornythwaite, Glaramara and Allen Crags to Esk Hause and Sty Head.

This walk differs from the other Sty Head routes in this section in that it doesn't start from Seathwaite, and unless you choose the long way back you will only see Sty Head from the mountain top. On the other hand, it is the only route in this book to take in Esk Hause, that friendly green meeting of the ways known to all who walk on the fells. The walk also differs from the others in that it is a true, high fell walk rising to over 2,500 ft at both Glaramara and Allen Crags, and like the Wasdale Head route you'd be wise to reserve for it the best part of a day.

Leaving Seatoller behind you, walk back along the main road towards Keswick as far as Mountain View Cottages and turn right into the entrance to Thornythwaite Farm. Here you do not proceed up the farm path, but instead climb the ladder stile over the wall on your left and follow the path immediately ahead, parallel with the Keswick Road. Don't worry, you are not going to scramble up that great mass before you; the path bears round to go gently upwards for about fifteen minutes, then through a wooden gate onto the open fell. Now you are beside Comb Gill, and the path goes straight south all the way to Esk Hause some 2½ hours away.

Once the path is cairned away from the rush and tumble of the beck you will find yourself in a near-silent world, the only sounds the song of the wheatears, stonechats and skylarks which accompany you. Thornythwaite is a green fell, cradled in green fells; it is cut off from the broad valley of the Sty by the high ground between, and not until you reach the summit cairn on Glaramara will you see Sty Head Gill winding along the valley bottom, incredibly far below. On the left as you go is the great hanging valley of Comb Door, well worth walking across to look at. Don't forget, too, to look back as you climb for the view of Rossthwaite and Seatoller, Derwentwater and Keswick in the valley behind you, with Skiddaw and Blencathra rising beyond.

Thornythwaite's secret world broadens into a plateau on the approach to Glaramara, and the path loses itself in a soggy patch, where you rely on the cairns to guide you. A little, clear beck crosses this bog which is worth remarking, as it is the last running water you will see until you get to Esk Hause, over an hour away. Soon after this you come to Glaramara peak, where the cairns direct you up a short cliff face; don't be daunted, it's an easy little climb and a few yards from the top is the summit cairn.

Here you are on top of the world; the hills surge to your feet like seas, Brandreth and Gable above Sty Head Gill with the Wasdale Fells to their left and Yewbarrow behind, coming round to Scafell and Scafell Pike ahead of you, and to their left again Esk Pike and Bowfell. The passes of Sty Head, Lingmell and Esk Hause are the troughs of the waves, Derwentwater and Skiddaw are behind you, and over all is the still, blue summer heat-haze. Enjoy it while you can, as the cairns will now take you, still due south, on a rocky path which seems to go on, up and down, for ever, until you pass at last between the twin cairns that mark the summit of Allen Crags. The approach to these cairns is dotted with pretty little tarns, and prettiest of all, just before you reach the summit, is the little gem of Lincomb Tarn caught in its deep basin of rock.

From the summit cairns on Allen Crags a trot down a welcome patch of green followed by a short scree run brings you in sight of the broad pass and shelter cross at Esk Hause where the signpost points the ways to Scafell, Angle Tarn, Seathwaite and Great Gable. At Esk Hause you turn right to take the north-west path which passes close by Sprinkling

Tarn on its way to Sty Head. If you are returning to Seathwaite by the easy route alongside Sty Head Gill, keep to this path until you reach the Sty Head signpost, then follow the gill as described in (4).

The route back by Grains Gill is quicker and more interesting, and only slightly more arduous. For this route you follow the path only until Sprinkling Tarn comes into view ahead right, when you will see, well this side of the tarn, another red path bearing off on the far side of the beck with which you have been keeping company since Esk Hause. Cross the beck by stepping stones and follow this path alongside Grains Gill back to Seathwaite as described in (1).

FOUR BORROWDALE VILLAGES from KESWICK,
using the Derwentwater boat service and the bus.

Approximate times for the various stages of the walk: to Watendlath from Ashness landing, 1½–2 hours; Watendlath to Dock Tarn and back, 1 hour; Watendlath to Rossthwaite, ¾–1 hour; Rossthwaite to Seatoller, 20 minutes; Rossthwaite to Grange & Lodore Landing, 1½ hours.

Sometimes the fell tops are shrouded in mist and a wise walker keeps off them; on such a day this pleasant low-level walk may be found ideal. It gives a ride by launch across Derwentwater, then goes by safe paths to the four tiny Borrowdale villages of Watendlath, Rossthwaite, Seatoller and Grange, that nestle like gemstones in the folds of the fells.

From Keswick town centre, follow the sign 'To the Lake' until you come to the jetty from which the passenger launch plies across Derwentwater. Alight at Ashness Landing and look for the single-track lane signposted 'Ashness and Watendlath'. The way winds up this lane for a mile or so in a long, steady climb around the foot of Ashness Fell, giving wonderful views over Derwentwater to Cat Bells beyond, and crossing on the way the famous Ashness Bridge seen on all the picture postcards.

After about twenty minutes the lane passes through a gate into the National Trust property of Ashness Wood, where it winds about in the shade until, having passed a large cairn on the left, it meets a broad track leading off on the right in a V fork. There have been several smaller tracks into the wood but this one is very obvious, almost a roadway, and has been marked by the National Trust Wardens with the single word PATH on a four-foot post. The route can further be identified by a clump of small pines at the wide entrance, and a passing place for cars opposite.

This path runs through the wood for about a quarter of a mile, coming close to Watendlath Beck which flows in a slight cleft below on the right. At a ladder stile over a wall it turns at a right-angle to cross the bridge over the beck, then left to follow beside the beck all the way to Watendlath.

It is lovely here beside the beck, winter or summer. Ashness Fell rises on the left, and to the right the path is enclosed by Grange Fell and the little crags of Caffell Side. Watendlath Beck, chuckling over its stones, abounds with birds – dippers and wagtails and friendly little coots – and its banks are scattered with wild flowers.

After a peaceful half-hour stroll Watendlath village is seen, no more than a hamlet scattered beside a tarn, and every house seems to offer teas and snacks. Whatever the weather, it is pleasant to sit at the door of one of the cottages sipping coffee and gazing out over the fells and the tarn, with no sound to break the peace save the tumbling of the beck over its bed and the occasional crowing of a farmyard cock. Continuing, the way crosses back over the stone bridge where Watendlath Beck meets the tarn to turn left onto the footpath signposted 'Rossthwaite'. Fifty yards on it leads through a gate onto the open fell and climbs a knoll ahead, where Rossthwaite is again signposted. There is a path here on the left to Dock Tarn, a mile away at the foot of Stonethwaite fell. The trip across to Dock Tarn is recommended, and will add only an hour or so to the walk. But before you proceed either to Rossthwaite or Dock Tarn, do pause at the top of the knoll to look back for a last glimpse of

Watendlath down in the valley, cradled in green hills.

As the way goes on towards Rossthwaite, Scafell and Scafell Pike can be seen rising ahead on the left, with Great Gable a little to the right of them and Glaramara in the foreground. Soon, too, the white houses of Rossthwaite come into view nestling in the dale where the path ends.

At Rossthwaite there is a village shop-cum-Post Office, and a pub for refreshments. Here you can wait for the bus back to Keswick or Grange, or turn left onto the road to walk a mile into tiny Seatoller, at the foot of Honister Pass. The Keswick bus terminates at Seatoller, where it waits five minutes before returning to Keswick.

Alternatively, a right turn onto the road at Rossthwaite brings one to the footpath to Grange. This footpath leaves the Rossthwaite to Keswick road on the left some half-mile from Rossthwaite village to cross the river Derwent and run in part through the wood and in part beside the river, coming out in the middle of Grange village. Here one turns right to re-cross the Derwent by the road bridge, then left onto the Keswick road for another mile to the boat landing at Lodore and the launch back to Keswick.